Love Wins:
5 Keys to
Strengthen Your
Relationships
A Parent & Child
Perspective

By Avery and Brian
Baker

Library of Congress Control Number: 2019907378

Cover photo by Diana Miller Photography
(dianamiller.com)

Cover design by Brandon McGinnis

For information about special discounts available for
bulk purchases, sales promotions, and educational
needs, contact Avery and Brian Baker at:
averyandbrianbaker@gmail.com

www.averyandbrian.com

THIS BOOK IS DEDICATED TO 3 GENERATIONS OF STRONG
MEN IN OUR FAMILY:

JAMES A. FRENCH (GRANDFATHER AND GREAT
GRANDFATHER)

RALPH F. BAKER (FATHER AND GRANDFATHER)

MARK F. BAKER (BROTHER AND UNCLE)

WITHOUT THEIR GUIDANCE, WISDOM, AND SPIRIT OUR
JOURNEY WOULD NOT BE POSSIBLE.

"THOSE OF US WHO HIT THE LOTTERY HAVE A RESPONSIBILITY TO HELP OTHERS WHO DIDN'T. PARENTS, A LOT OF WHAT HAPPENS TO YOU IS LUCK." -BRIAN BAKERISM

CONTENTS

FOREWORD

The book you hold in your hands is a treasure of many decades and four generations in the making. This book shares the "big reveal" of the work of a black family to raise good, strong sons/men. On the paternal side, it starts with a grandfather who decided as a very young man to be the best dad he could be, to be the dad that he himself wished for. On the maternal side, it begins with a great-grandfather who was an educator, community leader and world traveler.

I met the grandfather, Ralph Baker, thirty years ago when we began to work together. We were good colleagues and later we developed a brother-sister bond and Ralph adopted me into his family. Ralph was so proud of his sons Mark and Brian. When I first met them, they were young married men, building their families and careers. I observed how devoted Mark and Brian were to their wives, and they were each other's best friend. I watched Mark and Brian partner with their dad Ralph and maternal grandfather Avery French to raise Brian's sons, Avery and Justin. As I grew to know Mark and Brian, I loved and admired them, they were such outstanding young men!

I often pressed Ralph to share with me how he raised

such wonderful young men. Ralph was the consummate storyteller, and he would entertain me with stories about the Mark and Brian's escapades and their family life as the boys were growing up. He shared with me that he and their mother Maude were a balancing act in raising their sons. Ralph talked with me about how his father-in-law Avery was a wonderful grandfather to his sons; taking them on world travels, teaching them to be men of the world.

Over time, I began to really press Ralph to write a book to share his wisdom and insights on raising healthy black sons. I knew that their story needed to be told. I knew that we needed the Baker story as another counter-narrative to the prevalent story of black men as "absent fathers", "slacker dads" and "baby daddies". We needed their story as another counter-narrative to the prevailing stories of young black boys and men as drug users, pushers, drop-outs and gangbangers.

But I was pressing too soon! We know now that Ralph was not to tell the story about Mark and Brian. The story had to come from the next generation to include Brian's sons, Avery and Justin. With Avery and Justin there is another generation proving the wisdom and truths of their family life, demonstrating the love that undergirds it all. With third generation Brian and fourth generation Avery and Justin, Father and Sons together tell an even more powerful and compelling story. The story now has the benefit of both time and timeliness. Brian, Avery and Justin together tell how the family over time has shaped them. And it is timely because they share how they faced preparing Avery and Justin to take advantage of unprecedented opportunities for young black men against the backdrop of protecting them against the many predators that destroy so many of our young black sons and men.

What the Bakers have accomplished as a family is truly wonderful. But I must say that any black family can do what they have done. And that is the treasure in the book that you hold. The book contains the story of real black family life, not a perfect family, but a real family. I urge you to draw wisdom and encouragement to raise your own strong black sons. And when you do, turn and share your story, adding your own story to the counter-narratives to encourage the next generation of black families!

A final point, the black family is not complete without the strong black women who are the wives, mothers and grandmothers who have the love and wisdom to support their husbands and sons to be strong men. The women in the Baker narrative include Ralph's mother Portia, grandmother and great-grandmother to Brian and Avery and Justin; Maude, mother to Brian and grandmother to Avery and Justin, and Lynette, wife of Brian and mother of Avery and Justin. The stamp of each of these women is clearly on all of the Baker men.

Rose Owens-West, Ph.D.

Ordinary People, Extraordinary Relationships

"We are just ordinary people that have extraordinary relationships." -Brian Bakerism

Brian, Father

February 11, 2008. I'll never forget that morning. It was just a small moment in the morning of a day that changed my life forever. But then, we never really forget the days that change our lives forever, do we? Those moments that change us forever.

It started out like any other day in my life. I left the house a little early so I could get to the office with plenty of time to prepare for a weekly sales meeting. I settled in with a cup of tea and had just begun to review the sales reports when I got a call from George, a friend of my father's. He had been staying with my father to help him recover from a routine knee replacement surgery. The instant I heard his voice, I knew something was wrong. "What is it?" I asked. "Brian, your father passed away in his sleep." I couldn't process what he was telling me. In the blink of an eye, my life was changed forever.

Ralph F. Baker, or Pops, as I called him, was the greatest father a son could have. He was everything I strived to be. He was loving, intelligent, present, a good provider, thoughtful, understanding, a friend, happy, insightful, positive, and an optimist. It sounds like an impossible, superhuman list but I could keep going.

I'm grateful to my father for many things. His unconditional love and support, his sense of humor, and his steadfast ability to see the good in other people were hallmarks of a man who practiced what he preached. I'm particularly grateful for the behavior he modeled when it came to interpersonal relationships. The man knew how to build deep, lasting relationships with the people that mattered to him. Because of his example, I committed to be the best parent, the best husband, and the best human being I could be.

It wasn't easy to follow in his footsteps. In the span of just 23 short months, I lost my grandfather, brother and grandmother along with the loss of my father. It was the most difficult two years of my life. Family is everything to me and enduring such loss in a short amount of time left me without the solid foundation I had relied on for so long.

Without this foundation, I found myself struggling to be a good husband, father, friend and colleague. Before these losses, I was engaged and excited about life but after, I felt unmoored and alone. I grew distant and aloof. I stopped enjoying the things I once did and there were many days that I wished I could just remain unconscious. Essentially, I became a shell of my former self.

Luckily, those I loved, and loved me in return, viewed me through the lens of who I was prior to the loss of my family members. I say luckily because I didn't even like myself. During this dark time, a friend asked me if I had heard of a concept called "Emotional Intelligence." This was new to me and as I read about it, I was fascinated to learn that the basic concepts of Emotional Intelligence, or "EI", (self-awareness, empathy, communication, collaboration, awareness of others, etc.) were already familiar to me. These concepts were taught to me from an early age by my parents.

Because I witnessed my father's determination to build a strong foundation for our family, I was able to draw from his example and find the strength to slowly bring myself back to life. My father is the reason this book about having deeper, connected relationships is being written. He is the reason I recommitted to setting a solid foundation within my own family unit using the tools he gave me. Pop's wisdom and love are written between the lines of not only this book as well as in the lines of my very soul.

My son Avery and I are just sharing the tools.

Avery, Son

My parents always told me that my journey was uniquely my own. My father told me not to compare my journey, or, for that matter, myself, with anyone else. When you are told something your whole life, over and over, it tends to stick with you.

We were encouraged "To be better on Tuesday than we were on Monday." My father worked hard to give us a home where open communication and trust was valued and encouraged. Working together, my parents insisted on establishing a loving, accepting place for us to retreat to when times were hard. He and my mother set the example for me and my brother Justin and because of their hard work, we were lucky to enjoy a closeness that not many families experience.

This closeness wasn't always easy. It was great, but definitely not easy for me at times, especially when I was struggling to learn how to be independent. In our family, we were expected to be tuned into one another. We were taught to listen to what was said, as well as being mindful of what was not said. This fine attunement to one another did bring us close together, but to a young teen trying to figure out who I was, it could feel somewhat smothering.

I was in middle school around the same time our family suffered so many losses. The preteen and teenage years aren't easy under the best of circumstances and I saw my family, particularly my father, suffering. This had a profound impact on me. Being naturally non-confrontational, I retreated into myself. My father, a naturally affectionate person, was frustrated by my emotional absence. This led to some strife between us at a critical time in my life, because like everyone else my age, I was just trying to fit in.

At this age, society and environment began to have a greater impact on me. With this larger world, came the acknowledgement and identity of my own race, and what that meant to me, and what that meant to others outside my tightly knit family unit.

To say my parents valued education is somewhat of an understatement. Education was the main focus throughout my childhood. Because my birthday is in January, my parents could not enroll me early in kindergarten at the public school by our house, so I began my education in private schools where I was usually the only black kid in class. After a while, I became used to this and adapted. As I grew older, my parents decided I would transfer to public school for my middle school years. I was no longer the black kid in class. Now, I was now one of several black kids in my class. The newness was exciting.

However, this affected me in more ways than I would have imagined. First, I realized very quickly that I had been cast into the mold of a "stereotypical" black kid. Many of my teachers had low expectations of me in the classroom, while non-black students expressed how different I was from what their preconceived biases were.

To the other black kids, I carried myself differently and the differences didn't go unnoticed. I didn't wear sagging pants, largely because my father would whoop me if he saw me doing such a thing. My father always said, "Saggy pants equals a saggy mind." This quote is an infamous Brian Bakerism. Brian Bakerisms are phrases my dad created and used throughout my upbringing. They will appear throughout this book, just as they have throughout my life.

Also, the brothas and sistahs said I talked "white". In fact, my first girlfriend's best friend, who was black, actually called me "white boy" for the duration of the year. I was different from both blacks and whites at my new school and I felt these differences keenly and so did everyone around me. During the summer before my 8th grade year, a year that is now seared in my memory forever, I was playing the basketball game "Knockout" at a high school camp.

I bounced the basketball on the ground, gearing up to shoot. I paused for a moment before shooting. Behind me, I heard a voice say, "Hurry up, nigger."

It was jarring. I was embarrassed and I froze. I couldn't shoot.

Now maybe, if I try in retrospect to give him the benefit of the doubt, he said "nigga" in a misguided effort to be cool, but it made no difference to me. I had never been referred that way in my entire life, let alone by a white kid. This was new. It stuck with me.

During my freshman year of high school, I was in

accelerated classes and, again, I was one of a handful of black students in my classes. I also played basketball for the school team, where most of the other players were black. No matter which group or activity I set out to do, I struggled to find my place. Often, I dealt with "shade" from different groups of students. Asian, Indian, and white students automatically deemed me not smart enough to be in classes with them, and the black students said, "You're too good to be with us." This was a direct quote from a former teammate. It hurt.

This created a lot of anxiety for me. I love my African American Heritage, so it hurt to have other black kids diminish my blackness. The mantra I began to carry with me was, "Too black for the white kids, too white for the black kids."

But, you know, as difficult as that time was for me, it helped to shape me into the man I am today. At a time when children start to naturally test their autonomy, I was forced into becoming increasingly independent. I began to loathe the idea of group-think, because I belonged to no group. No group that is, except for my family and it was this group that had the greatest impact on me.

I love them so much for helping me through a rough

time in my life, even when I didn't ask for their help. They were my support system, even when I wanted to deal with it on my own. They emboldened me when I was lacking self-confidence. They gave me the tools to recognize where I belonged and most importantly, who I was.

We've dedicated our lives and careers to helping others deepen their bonds in their relationships. We realize that not everyone knows what it takes to create healthy relationships or even what they look like. Or perhaps, their relationships have fallen apart, and they yearn to put them back together.

If you want to create, grow or repair your relationship, this book was made for you. It's our sincerest hope that within these pages you will find the inspiration to make your relationships "Better on Tuesday than they were on Monday." If you find that there are some days you can do exactly that, we've done our job.

The Goal

"Closed mouths don't get fed." -Brian Bakerism

Middle school aged kids aren't exactly known for their communication skills. This isn't news to anyone, but like a lot of parents of middle school kids, my wife and I were taken by surprise when Avery's behavior began to markedly change. He had always been a happy kid and an excellent student, but it seemed like he was really struggling. He became withdrawn and his grades dropped. This wasn't normal for him and we were alarmed. There had been a few changes in his life. He had just transferred to a larger public school from a small, private school and we could see that the adjustment was a difficult one. We had expected an adjustment period, but this was different. Avery just didn't seem like himself, so we tried to get to the bottom of what was bothering him.

For months, we did all we could to help him. We helped him study, we met with teachers, we kept on him about the importance of being a good student. We were as involved as parents could be.

We asked him why he thought he was getting such bad grades after being an honor student. He didn't have an answer for us but that didn't stop me from asking him over and over again.

I can't leave a problem alone, and I especially can't leave it alone when I see my kid suffering. So, I thought I should ask again in case he had any new insights. And, so I did. I asked him and guess what? After asking for the umpteenth time, he still didn't have an answer for me. Avery became so anxious over this new situation that he would vomit from the stress.

One day, I called my father to talk about Avery. He quietly listened to me for a few minutes before asking, "Do you want to know what his issue is?"

Of course, I wanted to know. I wanted to know why he couldn't talk to me when all I wanted to do was help him.

He said, "The reason that he can't tell you what his issue is, because he doesn't truly understand it himself."

He then reminded me just how hard this time is in an adolescent's life and how difficult the transition to a larger school must be on him. He told me I needed to be patient for a while and he assured me that when Avery was ready, he would be able to talk to us.

"Avery is going to be okay," he said.

As usual, Pops was right. Avery got through it and the shaky ground he had seemed to be standing on for so long finally stabilized. He found his footing and began to relax and act like his old self.

In my eagerness to help my son, I hadn't chosen the right time to have a conversation, nor had I given Avery enough space to identify what was wrong. My natural inclination was to jump in and help. It's difficult at any age to discuss sensitive subjects and sometimes it seems almost impossible to someone so young. Evidently, I had lessons to learn, too, and I'm grateful I had my Pops to teach me that lesson. -Brian

Connecting Through Conversation

One of the hallmarks of a happy and connected family is their ability to have open conversations with one another. Honest and open communication within a family allows each member to express their needs and desires in an accepting space. Bonds grow when family members feel confident enough to open up and share their innermost feelings and issues. The issues all families will face are more readily resolved when there is healthy communication.

Increasingly, our society is reeling from the effects of a deep disconnect within our families. Youth suicides have steadily increased and while we can't point to a single factor, several studies have shown that disconnection within our families and social support groups is a powerful risk factor in youth suicide (Lakey and Cronin). When young people feel they don't belong or have a safe place to express their feelings, then hopelessness, isolation and desperation grow.

These feelings of isolation and desperation are eased by a feeling of connection. Feeling connected with others, especially our families, bring with it a sense of belonging, being heard and most importantly, understood. One of the best ways to do this is through genuine, caring exchanges. This type of communication doesn't always come naturally but like any skill, it can be learned.

Here are a few ways we can deepen the connections

within our families through healthier, open conversations:

Pay attention and listen

Listening, really listening, to our loved ones is the most important communication skill of all. Actively listening to our families deepens the love that binds us to one another. It builds trust as well as a sense of safety in our homes. We enjoy more positive relationships when we strive to hear what is being said to us rather than listening to merely respond.

Why is this?

It may seem like a no-brainer, but truthfully, just between us friends, how many times have we caught our minds wandering when someone is talking? Or, even more embarrassing, how many times have we been called out for not paying attention? It's obvious when someone isn't giving us their full attention, isn't it? It doesn't feel great to be on the receiving end of a one-way conversation like this and it can lead to feelings of mistrust if it becomes a pattern. Who wants to open up to someone if the other person can't do something as simple as listening to what you have to say? Without being actively engaged in our interactions, our relationships can become shallow and we can begin to feel disconnected with one another.

Here are some common listening mistakes we've all been guilty of from time-to-time.

- Preparing what you will say next or predicting what they will say next.
- Daydreaming of something else (i.e. what's for dinner, returning a text/call, YouTube clips, worrying about time, etc.).
- Judging what the other person is saying.
- Listening to the discussion with a specific outcome in mind.
- Fidgeting or defensive posture (unconsciously or consciously).

Cringing a bit? We've all done it, but here's how we fix it:

Active Listening

We've heard a lot about active listening over the years but it's important to remember that active listening is so much more than a trendy buzzword. And it's much more than sitting still, considerately refraining from interrupting or nodding politely while the other is speaking.

Active listening requires a genuine interest in what

the other person has to say. The subject doesn't have to interest you. The important thing to remember is that the person doing the talking does interest you and is important to you.

Active listening is sparked by a curiosity about what makes the other person tick and this sincere attention goes a long way in a relationship.

When we are on the receiving end of sincere attention, we are more comfortable opening up and being vulnerable. For children, this validates them and allows them to feel safe. This feeling of safety has huge payoffs down the road.

Admittedly, when the boys were younger, it was sometimes difficult to pay full attention to what they were saying. But, I made an effort to listen to them no matter what they wanted to talk about, and as many times as they wanted to tell me about it. Eventually, it paid off. As time passed and they grew up, conversations naturally became more interesting, but more importantly, they trusted us to listen to the big things because we had taken the time and listened to the little things. –Brian

Here are some ways to become an active listener:

- Pay attention to the one talking and not to your own thoughts.
- Be quiet but not silent. Some verbal and non-verbal feedback to show you're listening is important (i.e. leaning in, smiling, nodding, etc.)
- Ask a lot of open-ended, unbiased, neutral questions that lead the conversation in a positive direction.
- Build bridges of understanding and cooperation; seek out common interests and goals and speak to those.
- Seek first to understand what the other person is saying; ask questions to clarify (they won't hear you until you hear them).

Timing is everything

The timing of our conversations, especially difficult conversations, is just as important as learning to listen. All too often, we rush in because we are eager to get whatever we have to say off our chest. In our haste to express ourselves, we dump our feelings in one giant, messy pile at the feet of the other person. As a result, this can cause the other person to feel blindsided or unprepared.

When this happens, the other person might feel attacked. Naturally, this causes them to feel defensive.

and when one person in a conversation is on the defense, the conversation hits a brick wall. In fact, at that point, you may have more success talking with a brick wall than with someone you inadvertently alienated, even if we had the best of intentions. Brian learned this lesson the hard way:

When Avery was younger, I had the privilege of coaching his competitive basketball (AAU) team. For five years I loved this job and I took it seriously...maybe a little too seriously. In fact, I was so passionate about it that I made sure Avery was "lucky enough" to get the very best off the court "coaching" in the car on the way home from the games.

After a while, I realized that my off the court coaching was having the opposite effect of what I had intended. I had a captive audience and I took full advantage of the opportunity until one day I noticed that Avery was spending increasingly more time staring out of the window, diligently working on his 'ignoring abilities.'

It finally dawned on me that he just needed time to process things on his own—well, that and maybe some food, of course. He didn't need more coaching and he didn't need advice on how to polish his jump shot. Immediately after the game, cornered in a car, wasn't the best place to go over the highlights or lowlights of the game. What he needed was his father to take off his coach hat and put on his dad hat. -Brian

Deal with it

We may be tempted to put off conversations because we don't know how to bring the subject up. When it comes to difficult subjects, there is a lot of fear and trepidation in the unknown. Our imaginations run away with us and we become so fearful of possible repercussions that may stem from the conversation, we end up avoiding confrontation at all costs.

However, avoiding issues does come with a price. Actively ignoring the issues that weigh on our minds can have a big impact on our relationships. The resulting anxiety that comes from circumventing problems comes at a significant cost to our relationships. It can lead to an unhealthy pattern of suppression and denial and will cause stress, disconnect, and disappointment with a partner.

While important conversations shouldn't be put off indefinitely, there is a time and a place for everything. We should thoughtfully choose the timing of our delicate conversations and wait until the appropriate time presents itself. There is no hard and fast rule to use in determining the correct moment for these more sensitive issues. Only you can determine when the time is right.

Be available

One of the most important ingredients in having open and healthy conversations is availability. If open conversations are going to flourish, we must be present in the moment.

In this hyper-connected digital world of social media, voice mail, email, and texts, being physically present and communicating face-to-face is increasingly vital. One-on-one interaction does more to foster far deeper levels of intimacy than staring at the glowing screen in our hands.

Being physically present and available to connect on a more personal, human level is essential because most of our interactions with others are non-verbal. Words make up only a part of our interpersonal communications. The rest is composed of body language, facial expressions, and voice tone in order to give us true context and meaning. How many of us have misread the tone of a text or email? Or even missed the facial expressions of someone we were having a half-hearted conversation with because we were too busy in front of a computer monitor or watching a television show to look up?

We can't talk to our families if we are never around. Making a conscious effort to slow down the hectic pace of our busy lives allows us to connect with each other, but first we have to unplug! There is a time and place for our electronics, but we miss too many moments to connect with our families on a deeper level because we are too busy staring at a screen.

Be patient with one another

Conversations, especially the difficult ones, rarely go as smoothly as we hope. Conversations can take on a life of their own and no matter how carefully we plan them, they hardly ever go as we expect. We have all struggled to find the words to express ourselves and we have all struggled to be patient while our partners tried to find a way to express what they are feeling.

Every message we send during a conversation comes with a verbal and nonverbal message and we process these messages through our own personal filters. These innate filters come with our own biases and these biases paint our responses to each conversation we have.

It's important to be aware of these filters so that we aren't so rigid in our responses, or so rigid in our opinions. Rigidity shuts down conversations. We need to be able to move in response to the dialog and be fully invested in the moment. Stop planning our responses before our partner or loved one has finished sharing their perspective. When we do this, it creates a feeling of mistrust. We can all tell when we are really listened to and when we are not. Paying attention to what they are saying with sincerity and patience creates a sanctuary where sharing thoughts and feelings can thrive. Also, abandoning expectations for a particular outcome fosters a sense of security and freedom, which also builds a sense of trust.

Disagree with civility

Disagreements are uncomfortable. They can quickly turn a respectful conversation into a tense and angry situation. Learning to disagree with civility is an underappreciated art form and one that takes practice, especially when we feel challenged by the other person's point of view. When we disagree with someone and tensions run high, we can do a few things to turn a disagreement into productive dialogue.

Focus on the good

You may disagree with someone, but there is still room for respect. Look for the positive in their argument. This doesn't take anything away from you and goes a long way in building trust.

Use "I" statements

"You" statements often sound harsh and accusatory. By using an "I" statement, we show that the disagreement isn't personal. "I" statements also demonstrate a sense of personal responsibility without taking the blame.

For example:

"I hear what you're saying, and I am sorry I made you feel that way." Instead of, "You misunderstood what I said, and you always overreact."

Don't get personal

Whether perceived or real, nothing shuts down a conversation like a personal attack from someone we love and care for. Disagreements can be stressful but letting our emotions get the best of us is never productive and is no excuse for hurting a loved one. Focus instead on why we feel the way we do instead of insulting someone because of how they feel.

We shouldn't be afraid of putting in a little work when it comes to having open conversations with our loved ones because when we invest the time in our families and work hard to improve this vital skill set, the dividends are priceless. Our families will naturally become closer but the effects of a connected family, where healthy conversations are the norm are far-reaching. When we learn to connect and communicate with our family, we also learn to connect and communicate with the world.

The Foundation

"You're gonna make mistakes, just don't make life altering mistakes." - Brian Bakerism

When I think about stories of trust (and mercy) I reflect back to my freshman year of high school. To give you a little context, both of my parents were educators. My mother was an elementary school teacher and my father spent 40 years as a teacher, a principal and an educational researcher. To say that education was serious business in the Baker household is an epic understatement. Expectations were as high as my hormones that first year of high school.

Like it does every year, report cards came out. How does it always manage to sneak up on students? I opened it up and was shocked. I guess I knew I had been cutting up pretty badly, but this was bad.

I had four D's. Four of them.

Four failing grades that I had to carry home to my parents who lived and breathed education. I looked at the grades on my report card and saw my life flash before my eyes. How was I going to explain this to my parents? I couldn't.

I went home with the embarrassing report card. I think it weighed ten pounds. Now, my father happened to be on a business trip, but he was due to return that evening. Maybe I would get lucky.

I showed my mother the grades. She looked at it and then simply said, "You're going to the airport with me to pick up your father." This wasn't good. On the bright side, though, it did give me about four hours to get my plea together. I went to work on the best excuses ever invented by a teenage boy. I thought of every excuse in the book, and there were some magnificent ones, but at the end of the day, I knew there were no excuses to be had. I realized my father was about to lose all trust in me and I couldn't blame him. High school is the time where we all try to spread our wings and I had just clipped mine.

As we waited curbside for my father to arrive, I remember thinking my mother couldn't help me even if she wanted to, and then it dawned on me; she didn't really want to help me. The teacher in her was saying "What the hell were you thinking?" As my father approached the car, the lump in my throat felt like a baseball.

After we all greeted each other I quietly said, "I got my report card." I had decided it was best to get it over with as soon as possible. I handed him the bad news and waited.

I remember looking at the back of his head, bent over, carefully reading the offending document and thinking that he sure was taking a long time to snatch me out the back seat. He slowly turned around, looked me in the eye with a great deal of disappointment, and quietly said "You've got to do better than this. This is not who you are."

What? That's it? I get to keep my teeth?

I still felt panicked, but the feeling began to turn into something else. I sat in silence for a while trying to put together what happened. It was hard to find the right thing to say.

Even back then as a young, stupid kid, I realized that my father had just demonstrated empathy for me, and at the same time, trust in me, too. He had every right to go completely off on me, but he didn't. Instead, he knew I was struggling in my transition to high school and he trusted me to do better in the future by reminding me of my abilities.

Don't get me wrong, there were consequences. I was grounded forever, but I still had my life, so all in all I think that was pretty fair. And I knew one thing, I didn't want to let him down again. -Brian

Laying the Foundation

Building trust is the second factor we used to empower our family. Without trust, we lose our sense of connection and emotional safety in that relationship. We've all been in a situation where we aren't sure if we can trust someone. It certainly doesn't make you feel comfortable with that person, does it? And ultimately, if we aren't comfortable on that basic level, how can we have a successful relationship?

When we trust someone, we rely on them to do the right thing. Our confidence and trust in them grow when their actions demonstrate that you are important to them. When there is mutual trust and respect, our bonds grow deeper, and we can relax with the comforting knowledge that there is someone in this world that has your back. We as humans need each other, and we aren't really meant to go through this life alone.

The writer George McDonald said, "It is a greater compliment to be trusted than to be loved." This is especially true for families. With a family, love is seemingly instantaneously granted at birth, but in order to empower your family, trust must be reworked over and over again.

Trust begins early

We begin to teach children about trust from a young age, long before they can fully grasp the concept of it. Creating a supporting environment and following through on the promises we make to them, no matter how small, goes a long way in teaching children how to trust and be trustworthy. When we don't supply a supportive environment where children feel safe, they get defensive and act out. They lack the self-awareness to understand why they feel a lack of trust and also lack the vocabulary to express it. This causes feelings of anxiety. When we are consistent with our word, and begin with the basics, our children can relax and learn to trust others. Everyone, especially children, notice when someone is taking care of their basic needs.

I guess I realized I could trust my father when there was food on the table every night. Yes, this is something basic, but in all honesty, throughout my life he's given me lessons and tools just through his actions. When I was younger, he used to work a lot and would sometimes travel, but he was always there when he said he would be. He never put work before me, my brother or my mother and I really appreciated that. I respected and trusted him for it. -Avery

Be consistent and reliable with your word

The building blocks of trust are built brick-by-brick. Building trust begins by making your actions match your word. If it seems simple, that's because on a basic level, it is.

If we find ourselves with a growing feeling of discontent or mistrust towards someone else, it may be because we have replaced substance with empty words. We can feel it when someone who truly loves us says, "I love you." We know when they mean it. We see how their actions back up those words. We also know when those words are said out of a sense of duty, or even worse, routine.

We show our love not only through our actions, but also our body language. Saying, "I love you" while ignoring your partner or children's needs, makes them doubt the expression of love. Maybe your family doesn't say "I love you" often and that's okay. Some families aren't verbally demonstrative, but each family has their way of showing love. When we make sure to show love sincerely, no matter the way your family is used to expressing love, feelings of trust grow.

Conversely, managing our reactions honestly is also another way in which we build trust. Not everything in our families will be fun and loving. We will disappoint each other--a lot. When this happens, we have a choice: Express your feelings of disappointment clearly and honestly with compassion, or we can shut down. We can shut down in several ways. We can lose our tempers; we can give someone the cold shoulder. Maybe we even pretend like nothing is wrong but none of these reactions is an honest one. When we aren't clear and honest about our feelings of disappointment with our loved ones, we build invisible resentments. Really, when we think about it, is resentment ever truly invisible? Resentment has a palpable presence that's hard to ignore.

Explain your reasoning for decisions or behavior

We are apt to trust a decision if we understand the "why" behind it. It's easier to trust someone if we are confident that their motivations have our best interests at heart. Sometimes, that "why" is simply, "I love you. I've been here before. Trust my experience." Sometimes, it takes a lot more explaining, but when we give others the respect of an explanation, they are more inclined to trust us and our experience.

> All my life, my father has taught me lessons and shared his wisdom. Believe it or not, there have been some things that have actually come to fruition exactly the way that he said they would. I didn't believe it at the time but eventually, this allowed me to trust him even more. For example, when I was sixteen, I told my parents that I wanted to get a job. My father had enjoyed a successful career and he wanted to share his experience.
>
> He took me through the steps of finding and landing a job. He taught me how to go into a workplace, how to inquire about a job and then how to follow up. He also taught me how to go

through the interview process. I vividly remember the first day I went job hunting. I walked in the room ready to leave but my parents took one look at me and made me take off the jeans and polo shirt I was wearing. They sent me back to put on some slacks, a dress shirt and a blazer. I was mortified. I didn't want to walk out the house looking like that. After all, I was 16 not 26, but I did what he suggested.

I must admit, it only took me two days to land my first job, and that would not have happened had Pops not schooled me. -Avery

When trust is tested

Any relationship worth having requires integrity in order to flourish. Of course, no relationship is perfect. In almost any relationship, some violation of trust will occur. A broken agreement, no matter how big or small, whether the agreement is implicit or explicit, destroys trust.

Relationships can recover when trust is broken but first, we must consider the conditions and reasons that lead to the betrayal so that the process of healing can begin, and trust is restored.

Our ability to recover from a betrayal of our trust depends on a mutual willingness to work it out, forgive and move on. There isn't a one-size-fits-all plan to get a relationship back on track after trust has been broken, but there are a few guidelines that can help restore that broken trust.

Be honest

Honesty is the most important step when restoring trust and is the foundation for any successful relationship. We trust our loved ones to be forthright. When our partners and children trust us enough to let us know when something is wrong, or they are open with their feelings, we can build more faith in their words and actions. We can help our children to be forthright by teaching them to examine their own feelings and motivations before making a promise.

We need to also cultivate the same character strength in ourselves. When we commit to something we really don't want to, we are setting ourselves, and the person we committed to, for failure. Listen to your gut. It knows. We can feel when we agree to do something we don't want to do. If we aren't honest with ourselves, how can we expect it of others? We can practice being completely transparent while being gentle and kind in our honesty. There is no need to be cruel under the guise of honesty but the more open we can be, the less doubt will creep into our relationships.

Be patient

When someone breaks our trust, it's natural to feel disappointment and/or fear as a result of this betrayal. The fear often shows up masked as anger or frustration but reacting with anger shuts down conversations. When we stay open to conversations, we encourage the healing that comes after trust is broken.

As hard as it is, it's important not to take our children's betrayal of trust personally. They are learning about what it means to be a trustworthy person and like any aspect of our character worth cultivating, this one takes practice. If, and when, our trust is broken, we shouldn't despair. Instead, we should approach the situation as an opportunity to discuss the value of trust in the world and in your family. Keep the lines of communication open even after trust has been broken and listen to the other person with an open heart. We don't know what was in their heart, but if we endeavor to understand where they were coming from, we can do our part to restore trust. Trust runs both ways and the person who broke our trust, must be able to talk with us.

*"Im'ma say this one last thing, then
I'm gonna leave it alone" -Brian
Bakerism*

Once the issue has been discussed and any repercussions are understood, it's time to drop the subject and let the person begin to make amends. Rehashing the issue causes resentment and switches the focus to recriminations instead of restitution.

Create a roadmap for success

Make a plan to restore trust with your partner or child. Ask them what they think the best way to regain trust is and how to implement it. When we are the ones who have broken trust, it's important to know what the other person needs in order to begin to trust again.

Learning what behavior changes they need to see, and then applying them, is a major step in rebuilding trust. Less talk, more action!

Model trust with acceptance and willingness to trust.

The most effective way to teach trust, and earn it, is to model it yourself. Modeling trust involves keeping our word and managing our reactions when boundary lines are tested, and trust is damaged. Our partners and our children watch us and if we are defensive or holding back, they will do the same. If we can remain open and willing to trust, our connection to one another is strengthened and will allow us to weather the times when our trust is inevitably tested. When we trust each other with a spirit of generosity, we build our connections and commitment to each other. We build bonds that may bend and stretch, but when they're built on a strong foundation, they will not break.

The Overlooked Key to Healthy Relationships

"The habits you have at 25 are those you start at 15."
-Brian Bakerism

Avery had just passed his driver's test. His world had changed fast and in a big way. This milestone moment brought a whole new set of anxieties for his mother and me. If you've ever had a child drive, you know what I'm talking about. If you haven't, just wait.

If there's ever a time for setting expectations, this would be it. His mother and I had worked hard to make sure he knew what was expected of him, both at school and at home, but this was something new. This was much more than making sure he kept his room clean and got good grades. There was a lot more at stake and it was up to us to make sure he knew exactly what our expectations were and more importantly, why we expected it.

It was up to Avery to meet those expectations in order to keep the privilege of driving. For once, he excitedly agreed to them because to a teenager, driving meant freedom.

There were the usual requests of a new driver: "Stay in the area." "Go straight to your destination." "Let us know when you arrive and when you leave so we know when to worry." "Buckle your seatbelt." "Ask permission to drive friends around." "Don't listen to music too loud because you need to concentrate."

All of these instructions were important, and they were probably exactly like every other expectation that parents make on the new driver in the house. There was, however, one crucial expectation that might be slightly different than other households, and it had to do with being pulled over by cops.

Now, all parents have probably carefully instructed their newly minted drivers on exactly what to do when or if they are pulled over — pull over safely, have your license and insurance ready, and be respectful. In our family, we went further.

You see, in the African American community, we worry about how our children are perceived by some police officers. We know the history of African American young men having interactions with police and somehow ending up shot and killed. And while police officers have one of the most difficult jobs in the world and they want to get home to their family at the end of the day, we want to make sure our sons get home as well. Our fear was that officers don't know how great of a kid Avery is, so we needed to carefully coach him on what to do if he is pulled over. There is a "talk" that takes place in African American homes about interaction with law enforcement that many other communities don't have or even feel the need to have. My father had the talk with me and my brother, and we had the talk with our boys.

We instructed him to pull over immediately, if he ever found himself in that situation. Then, after he has stopped, we told him to turn on the overhead light so the officer could see both of his hands on the wheel. We didn't want him to reach for his wallet or to open the glove box to get his paperwork until instructed to do so. Then, he was to let the officer know what he was reaching for, because we knew this could be misinterpreted as reaching for a weapon. We told him we expected him to speak respectfully to the officer — not that we thought he would have been disrespectful, but this was different. We needed to stress this point. Avery was a kind, well-mannered kid but a police officer wouldn't know that.

We also told Avery that he couldn't have anyone else in the car that wouldn't uphold the same expectations we had of him. We weren't going to take a chance that one of his friends would mouth off at the officer and create a bad situation for everyone involved.

Avery agreed to the expectations and willingly followed them. It was a long time, however, before he was comfortable setting and enforcing the expectations on his friends. There was a long stretch of time when he wasn't allowed to have anyone in the car with him besides his younger brother Justin. Eventually he learned how to set expectations with his friends and was able to have friends in his car.

Just like Avery discovered, it's not always easy to set expectations. It's easy to assume that others will know what we need or how to behave but we aren't mind readers. We hope that others have our best interests at heart but when it comes to relationships, being clear is always best. The situation may not be as dramatic as a life at stake, but without clearly set expectations, our relationships could be at stake. -Brian

Here are some things we've learned about setting expectations:

Why set expectations?

Expectations for our relationships are deeply personal and often uncomfortable for us to talk about. A lot of us try to avoid talking about uncomfortable things. Without the ability to set and communicate our expectations in our families, our relationships may grow rocky, as unspoken and unmet expectations begin to fester. We would do well to remember that our personal expectations are just that–personal. We may share the same family goals, the same love for one another, and even the same genes, but what we expect from our relationships differs greatly from one another. Learning to communicate what is important to you and setting reasonable expectations around those things is the third key in building a committed and connected family.

We can probably agree that most of us are naturally good people with good intentions. No one sets out to do deliberate damage to a relationship, especially when we have invested so much of our time and hearts into them. We all strive to do the best we can for those we love. However, in a relationship where expectations are absent, we are forced to move through life and make decisions according to our own world view. In short, we assume. And we know that too often, what we assume isn't necessarily what the other person had in mind.

Sometimes, it's difficult to set expectations in our relationships. We may not want to rock the boat for fear of upsetting the other person. Or, we may not even know how to express our feelings in a productive way, but learning how to set expectations is vital to a healthy and happy family.

Setting expectations creates a sense of freedom

Hey now, hold up. Just how exactly can setting expectations create freedom?

Setting expectations sounds like another term for making rules, right? And rules mean restrictions. And restrictions sound more like a jail term or the fine print on a rental car policy. It certainly doesn't sound like freedom. But setting expectations in our relationships allows our bonds to grow deeper.

Here's how it works:

Pleasing those we love is one of life's greatest pleasures and the positive feelings that come from this strengthens our bonds. It's gratifying to see the smile of a loved one when we meet a need. On the flip side, when expectations go unmet, it silently erodes the trust that relationships need to thrive. Resentments grow and we doubt our importance to the other person.

When we communicate our expectations and see them being met, trust and mutual respect deepens our connection. Communicating what we need and expect from our families, with the knowledge that we will be taken seriously gives us a sense of security. We are assured that the time we've invested in the relationship has been time well-spent.

Expectations and deal breakers are not necessarily the same thing. Sometimes they are treated the same, but this usually happens when we aren't having the right conversations. How can we really know the difference if we are not open and honest in our discussions on the subject? If we can't tell one another if an expectation is a deal breaker, the lines blur until both parties are stubbornly in their own corner blaming the other for the breakdown that inevitably occurs.

We are human and we are going to let people down from time to time, but it's not the end of the world. We need to be flexible with others in the same way we want them to be flexible with us. Most importantly, we need to learn the difference between expectations and deal breakers so we can prioritize and place the proper emphasis on the expectations that matter most.

Expectations vs. deal breakers

Every single one of us has an internal code or set of rules that we live by, and that we expect the others in our families or relationships to live by. Expectations are entirely separate from deal breakers. Deal breakers are, at the most basic level, our own personal lines in the sand. These are beliefs and values that we carry with us into each relationship and you get to decide what these are. It's important that you know what these are for yourself.

If these lines are crossed, trust is eroded and the relationship is damaged, so being clear about your deal-breakers is not only important to a healthy and happy relationship, but only fair to everyone involved. Remember, only you can decide what your expectations are and which of them are deal breakers.

Here are some examples of both:

Deal Breakers:
- Lying/cheating
- Name-calling
- Physical Violence
- Stealing

- Gaslighting
- Substance abuse

Expectations:

- Help around the house
- Financial contributions
- Getting good grades
- Answering phone calls or texts promptly
- Knowing where your children are and who they are with
- Weekly family date nights

Recognizing and honoring our partner's deal breakers, or "relationship values" helps deepen our bonds with one another. Just like anything of profound importance, sometimes talking about our personal values isn't easy, especially if there has been a betrayal in the past. Discussions around these points should be approached with civility and respect. Tread lightly when there has been prior harm or disappointment.

We should also remember that children have deal breakers, too. It's easy for parents to have the trust of their child — after all, they are born trusting us to care for them, but sometimes, we can lose that trust. As a parent, trust is sacred. Children naturally want to work hard to earn your respect but they will shut down when their own innate set of values are broken. With the proper mindset and willingness to maintain a dialog of open and loving communication, keeping that sacred trust takes effort, but that effort yields magnificent dividends. So, how can we make sure these bonds aren't stretched or broken?

Practice setting expectations early (and revisit them often)

Setting expectations early on establishes a standard for both parties in a relationship. This can be with our children, or with our partners, or even with colleagues. Children especially thrive with the security that comes with clearly defined and healthy expectations. As parents, we can best model a loving relationship by acting with love towards those we love. This allows children to develop healthy and realistic expectations for their relationships.

"I don't care what other parents' kids can do; other kids aren't my kids."- Brian Bakerism

Be clear with your expectations, but if they aren't met, be understanding

Healthy, properly formulated expectations serve as a foundation for emotional intimacy and trust. If we are clear about our needs and wants in our own mind, we are better able to communicate them to our family. We can avoid resentments that are simmering on the back burner until one day, they boil over and disaster strikes. It's always easier to catch the pot before it boils over than to clean up the mess it makes.

Sometimes we hesitate to communicate our expectations because we are worried that it may alienate someone we care about. Figuring out what is important to you and your family, and why it's important, will make talking about your expectations a little easier. No family is the same. Every family has its unique quirks and rules to live by, but everyone should know what is expected of them.

I felt like it was important that if my kids were going to have expectations of themselves, then they needed to learn at a very young age what that meant. From the get-go, we wanted to make sure that when our kids looked in the mirror in the morning, they liked what they saw. I wanted them to expect something from the person in the mirror. We hoped this reflection was one of self-confidence and high self-esteem. Part of my reason for putting high expectations on our children was to make sure that self-worth was built into them from a young age.

If one of the boys brought home an 88% or 89% on a paper, I would be sure I congratulated him. If I suspected he could have done a little better, I held off telling him until a more appropriate time. I didn't immediately say, "You could get a 91%!"

I might say, "Great job dude" and then, later over dinner, I might ask them what they thought they could do to improve for next time. "Okay, now let's push a little bit." I would urge them. This was my way of saying to them that I knew if they put a little bit more work into it, better things could come out of it. The outcome might not be a better grade, but I tried to teach that putting in your best effort would be worth it. And, that's what I really wanted for them in school. I wanted the best for them, and to encourage them to strive for greater success and to want the best for themselves. I knew it was important to have them set their own expectations, rather than a parent simply telling them they expect better.

I felt that it was important, as young African American males, to have high expectations for themselves. Oftentimes, situations come about where people don't expect lofty things of you because of the color of your skin. Children of color will sometimes find themselves in a situation where they could be minimalized or marginalized. It was important to me that my kids thought highly of themselves from the beginning.

I also remember telling my kids this:

You have two names. You have a first name and a last name. The first name is yours the last name is all of ours. So, when you walked out of the house, I expected the Baker part of your name to be represented well and to exhibit the home training that you were given.

Those of us that have worked in corporate America know how focused we need to be on our job objective, and how our key performance indicators are measured. Many times, my boys didn't know what they were expected to do or how they would be measured so naturally they floundered a bit. They needed to have more defined expectations around their performance, and clearer job objectives so they could reach their goals. It was my job as a parent to help them learn to manage these expectations." –Brian

When it comes time to set expectations, there are a few things to remember.

First, make sure you are clear about your own expectations

What do you really want? Before speaking, take the time to be clear about your own goals so that you can communicate effectively. We also need to be clear about why we have our expectations. Taking the time to explain the "why" behind an expectation always yields better results than simply dictating the "how." This principle is often forgotten because when we find ourselves setting expectations for others, we tend to speak from a position of expertise.

We already understand how to do what we are requiring, so we tend to go straight to explaining the mechanics of the task or action we want accomplished. Of course, this is important, but this tact alone generally leaves gaps in true understanding. If we take the time to clearly communicate why an action needs to take place after we show someone how to do it, it is much easier for the person receiving the instruction to buy into the concept. This is because they can better see how following the progression steps will yield a positive outcome and the desired result.

Set aside an appropriate time to discuss your expectations

If it's important enough for you to talk about, then it is important enough to find an exclusive and appropriate time for the discussion. If your partner or child is hungry, cranky, or busy, they will not be in the proper frame of mind to really hear and understand you.

Keep it simple

There's no need to complicate expectations. Keeping it concise and positive makes it easier for the other person to be receptive to your needs.

Expect differences in opinion

Others may not agree with you or understand why you have certain expectations, and that's okay. Your expectations may not be theirs, but it doesn't mean it's not important to discuss. Differences of opinions are merely opportunities for growth and understanding in relationships--so is meeting an expectation that is important to our loved one, even if we may not agree.

Make sure your expectations aren't expressed or interpreted as demands

Communicating your expectations in a positive and approachable way helps the other person to remain open to meeting your needs. Demands on others will often be met with resistance, even if your intention is good or beneficial to the other party.

Defenses go up if the other person feels imposed upon, and the conversation will shut down. If an expectation is important enough for you to talk about, encourage all parties to be open-minded and approach how you express your expectations in a positive light.

Get agreement and commitment

Relationships are partnerships. They aren't one-way streets.

When we love someone understanding their motivations becomes important. When we care about the other person, we are anxiously engaged in making sure their needs are met.

Unmet expectations can cause hard feelings and the resulting bitterness can drive a wedge in any relationship. If expectations go unmet and resentments begin to simmer, take a moment to pause before reacting. Here is an opportunity to dig out the root cause and to spark open conversations.

These conversations take considerable trust and help us to draw closer to each other. If we don't have conversations about our expectations, we can miss subtle, but important, clues that the other person may not agree with us. Too often, we assume the other person is on the same page until an expectation is ignored or mishandled. If this happens a lot, resentments occur. Making sure there is an understanding of everyone's expectations benefits the family.

In order to effectively communicate your own expectations, first, you must listen to what your partner needs and then find out what they think about your expectations.

Pay attention to their body language and facial cues. Ask yourself: Does what I am observing tell me we are on the same page? Second, make sure anyone you share your expectations with understand your "why." Children, and even adults, have a hard time seeing the big picture but it's important to help them know your reasoning. Make sure you've presented it in a way that helps them to understand. We are all more apt to meet expectations if we know the reasoning behind it.

Expectations sometimes requires compromise

Everyone has a different set of expectations and every successful relationship requires compromise. As we now know, there is a difference between deal breakers and expectations. Expectations can be compromised when we discover they no longer work in a current situation. At its core, healthy compromise is a measure of how much one is willing to give or take for the good of a relationship, or the happiness of the other person.

Learning to compromise is not always easy, but we can learn how while staying true to ourselves.

Here are a few parameters to determine how much to compromise:

- Will I be happy if I compromised on this expectation?
- Do I feel that I haven't compromised what is important to me?
- Can I be satisfied with the new parameters?
- How much am I willing to compromise?
- If the other person isn't willing to budge at all and wants to drop it, would I be okay with that?
- If I'm not willing to compromise, am I comfortable enough to discuss my expectations and needs?

Sometimes, we try to avoid rocking the boat so much that we end up not making any progress at all, or we end up full of silent resentments but setting expectations is worth the momentary feelings of discomfort. Speaking of feelings, we might do well to remember that they are just that--momentary. Feelings are changeable, even malleable, but they don't give an honest representation of our actual relationship. However, expectations don't often drastically change because they are a basic part of what we need in a relationship, so making sure our expectations are understood and met is an invaluable key in building and maintaining happy relationships.

I was a good student and things came fairly easily to me. Growing up, I would get good grades in school and feel pretty good about myself. When I got an 88% or something like that, I would take it home to show my dad. He was supportive when he first saw my grade and he would congratulate me on it. Then, later, he would say something like, "So you couldn't get a 91%? Couldn't get an A-?"

Wow. Really, I thought I had done well.

But I didn't see where he was coming from. I was happy with the 88%. It wasn't hard to do, and I was content with skating by like that. The teachers didn't mind, so why should I?

Pops, though? He had other ideas for me. He knew I could do better, and he encouraged me to be better.

My father also had expectations when I wanted to go hang out with friends. It was never as simple as, "Hey I'm going to go over to so and so's house and we're just going to hang out maybe spend the night."

Oh no, no, no. It's not that simple. My father had to know everything. Everything.

"Where do they live? Who are their parents? What is their phone number and address? I need to know how you are getting there and if you are spending the night. Do I need to come get you in the morning?"

And on...and on...and on.

There were times where I would just say, "No, I can't hang out." before I even asked my parents. I knew the expectations of my parents and it was easier to say no right away, especially if I knew I was going to get denied.

But, you know, at the end of the day, because of these challenges, my parent's expectations have helped me become more of a strong-willed person and a critical thinker. I know how to make decisions effectively and how to set my own expectations of others. I am thankful for that even if I didn't understand exactly why they set those expectations for me from such a young age. –Avery

The Contract

*"Don't be a masterpiece of minimalism." -Brian
Bakerism*

Avery and I stood across from each other in the kitchen. It was August, right before his freshman year of college. Man, let me tell you, it was tense. At that moment, we were divided not just by the wide expanse of the kitchen island but by an even wider gulf of anger. Any other disagreement that had come before this paled in comparison to the rift we faced now.

Avery had graduated high school at seventeen and, like a lot of graduates, was eager to spread his wings. He had applied to several colleges and had gotten into some schools both close to home and away. We'd had a family discussion about finances and had come to the conclusion that it was best to stay close to home and attend the local university. We reasoned that if he lived at home his first year, his main focus would be to just go to school, focus on his grades and save up the money he made at his part time job. We would cover his car insurance and pay his tuition. We had planned for it and were excited to do this for him.

Boom. Decision made. Our son was going to college!

But, like a lot of seventeen-year-olds on the cusp of greater independence, things began to slip. As the summer progressed, Avery began to get a little "out of pocket" as we say. He started challenging things a little more. There were rules in our house. There were always rules in our house. He had chores, just like everyone else, but this summer he bent the rules. He started staying out past curfew and ignoring our text messages when we asked where he was and if he was okay. We started to butt heads and he started to get really cocky. I guess you can say he felt like he was a man at that point—and it's true, he nearly was. But the reality was that he was still being supported by us and we expected him to keep up his end of the bargain.

It all culminated that August morning. I was on one end of the island and he was on the other. The distance seemed too wide to be breached. We argued and he suddenly blurted out, "Well, I'm ready to move out."

Yeah, well guess what? I thought to myself. I'm ready for you to move out, too.

My wife was out of town visiting relatives, so I called her and told her about the blow up. I hung up and went to talk to Avery.

"By the end of the day, I'm going to give you some ultimatums."

This wasn't something I decided lightly. I knew if he moved out, there would be repercussions that would affect him, but this was a teachable moment. My wife and I were trying to give him the best start possible.

We also knew we had to continue to teach him how to uphold his end of the bargain. We had tried hard to raise a critical thinker. This made him an independent thinker and we were proud of that. I'm an affectionate father and I wear my heart on my sleeve. Giving my son an ultimatum was internally very difficult. It hurt to have a disagreement on any level with my boys, but I knew that was part of life as a parent.

Later that afternoon, I presented him with two contracts.

One contract was for if he chose to stay at home. In

this one, he would need to maintain a GPA of at least 3.5. If he didn't, he would have to take out school loans to pay for school the following semester and then he would also have to pay for his own cell phone data (parents, you know this battle) and he would have to begin to pay his own car insurance.

The second contract was for if he chose to move out. We agreed that we would pay rent only at one particular place and only as long as the above conditions were met (GPA, pay cell phone data, etc.). If he moved out, we would remove him from our car insurance, because we would be taking his car away. He would also be required to pay for his own food since meal plans did not come with his rent. He would always be welcome to eat at the house when he visited, though. *See the end of this chapter for an example of the contract.*

I told him he had 48 hours to decide and I waited.

And I wondered. What would he do?

During this time, I heard him on the phone to his Nana, and his family, and his friends asking for advice and to see if he could crash with them.

So, I waited. Then at the 47th hour, dude finally came

to me with his decision.

He agreed to stay and play by the rules. He wasn't too happy about it, and perhaps he was even a little resentful, but the critical thinker in him had carefully weighed the pros and cons and decided that staying at home would give him the best advantage.

We both learned lessons during this process. I wanted nothing but the best for him and my natural inclination was to talk about it over and over until it was resolved. I hated the temporary division in our relationship but the lessons we learned about conflict management were invaluable.

Our experiences leading up to that moment helped to prepare us and allowed us to come away from that experience with our relationship intact. -Brian

Conflict is inevitable.

Especially when it comes to our family dynamics. Have you ever known a family that didn't experience some sort of conflict? Neither have we.

But, listen up. Conflict isn't always a sign of dysfunction. Though conflicts can't ever be called "fun," healthy disagreements can be a way for us to grow together and learn more about our loved ones. Conflicts are just opportunities in disguise. Perhaps if we look at conflicts as a way to help families grow closer to each other, some of the sting of our disagreements will be lessened. In the process, we can learn more about the ones we live with and love.

Imagine how relationships would transform if we tweak the way we approach the inevitable conflicts, viewing them as those opportunities in disguise instead of arguments to win. Tweaking our approach to conflicts, can have profound effects on the outcome. This is great when you find yourself having the same argument over and over again.

However, if we avoid conflicts, and it's easy to do, resentments can develop, causing us to withdraw from our loved ones. We see this in some families where long-standing feuds create sharp divides that are increasingly difficult to bridge as the years progress.

And again, through lots of trial and error, we are excited to share what's worked for us. It wasn't always easy but here are some of the hard-won high points.

Focus on the issue or problem and do not make it personal

Conflicts are emotional and messy. They are usually accompanied by feelings of anger, frustration and disappointment. Our families and relationships are where we look for validation, love and acceptance, so when conflict arises, and we know it will, we feel vulnerable. Our hurt feelings put us on the defense because we are protecting ourselves. These feelings of vulnerability often aggravate the conflict and make it more difficult to solve. No one wants to be poked where it hurts. If we learn to pay attention, it will be easy to spot when someone we love is feeling vulnerable because they go on the defense. They may say hurtful things, things they know will hurt you and cut you to the quick.

Or maybe, if you take a deep dive into your own responses to conflict, you do this as your defensive mechanism as well. This is a natural human response. Just like we carefully hobble on an injured ankle, we intuitively protect our vulnerabilities when our feelings are hurt, and where are we more vulnerable than with the people we share our lives with?

If our conflict "auto-reply" is a defensive snap back, we risk the other person shutting down and ending the conversation.

Define the problem and make sure all parties agree on the core issue

Taking a moment to pause and understand what the core issues are goes far in resolving our disagreements with one another. Are you both on the same page? Do all parties agree on what the core issue is or are you arguing about completely different things?

Anyone who has been in an argument knows this happens a lot, but when we are in the thick of a tense situation, and harsh words are being flung around the room, it's hard to remember this small fact. Make sure you are on the same page first, then go from there.

Stick to the topic and refrain from bringing up others

Past disagreements should be left exactly there, in the past. If for some reason they haven't been resolved, pick it up at another time. Old disagreements should never be used as more ammunition for an argument. Stick to the topic at hand and focus on what is important in that moment. Piling on issues from the past makes mountains out of molehills and stirs feelings of resentment.

Put yourself in the other person's shoes

Understand that not everyone reacts the same way as you do and not everyone feels the same as you do. Work to sincerely understand what the other person is trying to convey to you and what they are feeling about the subject you aren't agreeing on.

Put yourself in their shoes. It will take you farther in your understanding than anything else.

No blaming or throwing stones

Families are always a "we" and never just a "you." There's no faster way to shut down a conversation than blaming or throwing stones. We never want to hurt the ones we love but all too often, we do when we place blame or toss around accusations. When two people are in the middle of a conflict, it's tempting to point out what the other person has done wrong and why they are responsible for the whole argument. It's too easy to become laser-focused on what the other person has done to make you feel the way you do.

When you place the blame solely in their court, you are making yourself the victim in the conflict. Hey, maybe in a way you are. Maybe the other person was totally out of line. They deserve to be called out on it, but it can be done in a way that won't put them on the defensive. This is hard to do when there are hurt feelings. These are some conflict patterns we find ourselves in way too often. You know those patterns, the same ones where one of us plays the victim and the other is on the defense. Maybe the roles are switched depending on the scenario, but they are the roles we automatically default to.

Seeing yourself as a victim means you are no longer a team. It means you've dropped the idea of two people working towards a solution together and want the other person to know they are wrong. There's an inherent lack of ownership when you play the victim. Stop the cycle but pay attention to where that feeling comes from. The feeling of powerlessness may lead to the root of the conflict. And when you have the root, you can solve it.

Remember, resolving conflict can be tricky. There is the potential for a situation to escalate and become more volatile if people we interact with are not willing to calmly work toward a resolution. If at any time you feel unsafe as you address problems in your relationship, please seek professional help. There is help out there and we have some resources in the back of the book if you need a place to start.

Address issues or potential issues in real time

Sometimes when we are feeling hurt or other strong emotions, we retreat into ourselves and withdraw from the other person. We may do this because we are feeling vulnerable or maybe we aren't comfortable with any sort of confrontation, so we sweep it under the rug to be dealt with at a later time. Maybe we are even hoping the other person will forget all about it and things can go back to normal. For little things, this isn't such a bad idea. Not every disagreement is worth fighting over. However, sweeping things under the rug, especially big things that are causing hurt feelings, can cause resentment.

Addressing the big things in real time is another way that we show how important our relationships are. Of course, waiting until both parties are calm enough to have a reasonable discussion is a good idea. Be assertive but kind with what your needs are. While you work through things, remain approachable and open to discussion about the conflict.

Be approachable

For the best possible outcome, it's imperative to be approachable when resolving conflicts. When conflict arises and we are hurt, we tend to retreat behind our defenses and snarl at anyone who dares to approach.

Nothing shuts down a conversation faster than making a few tentative gestures at reconciliation or conversation and having them soundly rebuffed. Making sure we are approachable allows us to take the first few steps in resolving conflict.

Give the benefit of the doubt

After all, we are a family. This is who we have chosen to live with and love. Shouldn't we assume the best in those we love? Be wise, but give them the benefit of the doubt, until they prove otherwise. And if they do disappoint us, and they will, forgive and do it all over again.

Remain calm

Yes, even when you are upset. Or hurt. Or angry. Or anything else. If you remain clam, it will help others keep calm. Conflicts bring out the worst in almost all of us. It takes self-control, respect and maturity to keep calm when everyone is upset. Raised voices, uncontrollable crying, and sarcasm only serve to shut down conversations and will do nothing to help resolve conflicts. If anything, it creates more animosity and defensive feelings. Losing control creates even more issues to solve as focus shifts to the outburst instead of the issue at hand.

Be aware of nonverbal communications

As we learned earlier, our bodies do a lot of talking for us. When we are knee-deep in conflict, be mindful of what we are unconsciously saying to our loved one. Are our arms crossed? Are we looking away? How about our eyes? Are they rolling in response to what we are hearing? Are we sighing or huffing in frustration? When we do this, we are speaking our feelings of anger and frustration loud and clear. Our bodies will say things that we sometimes feel like we can't, but we can use the responses we observe in others to help us resolve conflicts.

First, we need to be aware of what these subtle clues mean. Does the eye rolling mean that you feel misunderstood? Do our crossed arms mean we are feeling scared and/or vulnerable? Do our sighs mean we want to move on from the conversation? Don't leave it to chance that you will be understood. Tell them exactly how you feel. Let them know you are eager to solve your disagreement.

When we extend this awareness of these unconscious signals to the other person, we can take the fight out of them. No one likes to be on the receiving end of an angry teenager's dramatic eye roll. Or the cold shoulder of somebody pouting. These non-verbal cues can instantly create our own feelings of anger and frustration but if we address the issue itself, and not the physical reaction (which can be addressed at a later time when feelings are calm), we show a deeper generosity of spirit and this sets the stage to lovingly end our conflicts.

What does it really mean to agree to disagree?

"Okay, fine. Let's just agree to disagree."

These words carry both positive and negative connotations. When a discussion seems to come to a standstill, it's usually because both parties can't come to an agreement.

"Let's just agree to disagree!" is usually said with frustration because you both just can't seem to see eye-to-eye. It doesn't allow conversations to progress but there are benefits to recognizing that that it's time to stop the conversation.

Though this phrase is usually said in a moment of frustration, but there are positives to it. Conversations aren't often successful when emotions are running too high. Frustration turns to anger with lightning speed if we aren't paying attention to the root of the issue. If we feel that anger is building and the understanding is at a standstill, agreeing to disagree offers a way to salvage the conversation for a later time, when emotions are less raw. It allows us a timeout of sorts as we gather our thoughts and consider how better to approach the subject.

Think of it like a mutual white flag. It's simply another way to acknowledge that the relationship is more important than the disagreement and that the issue can, in fact, be put to bed forever, with no hard feelings, and, more importantly, with no repercussions.

To truly move on and use this phrase effectively, it's important to focus on what you really can control and forget the rest. This may be easier said than done. If you sense that the other person is only walking away out of frustration and the issue cannot be laid to rest, ask yourself a few things:

- Do I understand their point of view?
- Have I sincerely tried to put myself in their shoes?
- Have I been approachable, or have I been defensive?

After you've asked yourself these things, ask them, "What makes you want to stop now?"

After that, stop and listen. Make sure you are open to

what they say. You might hear something you don't want to hear but it will be information you can work with. Here are some of the things you might hear in response:

- "You aren't even listening to me. I hate talking to you."
- "You are so stubborn."
- "This is a complete waste of time."
- "If we keep talking, we will do permanent damage (i.e. breakup, estrangement of parent and child, etc.) "
- "I just need a break."

Some of these things are difficult to hear without feeling defensive. This is okay. Realize you are feeling defensive and work with those feelings to further the conversation. The other person may be responding to your defensive posturing, even if it's unconscious.

Having your shortcomings called to your attention, while not comfortable, is a great way to resolve conflict. If you notice defensive behavior for either party, you can bet that one or both of you is protecting vulnerability. It's often through conflict that we uncover our true selves, whether we like it or not. This is progress. This is intimacy. And that is exactly why we are putting in all of this hard work.

Forgive

Sometimes conflicts require forgiveness when they are done. Learning to forgive, and be forgiven in return, is an essential skill that must be learned before truly moving on from the conflict. Sometimes, the word "forgiveness" is offered up as a way to smooth over a tense situation, or perhaps forgiveness is withheld as punishment. If resentments or issues aren't properly addressed, then true forgiveness can't be given.

Move on and drop it

The inability to forgive and move on becomes our own personal prison of resentment. If we keep revisiting the issue after all the work we put in to resolve it, we never let the wound heal. Instead, it festers and becomes a bigger problem as resentments begin to pile on, one after the other, until we break down. If you have truly resolved the issue, drop it. Move on. If not, work on it. Or take a break. And then work on it again later. Our relationships are worth it.

Avoid behaviors that may trigger the resentments to resurface

This is simple. You probably already know exactly what will set off the other person. You know what buttons to push. Don't do that. What is "the moral of this story?" After the conflict is resolved, take a moment to ponder what the disagreement was really about. It's never about a messy room when your child is six and it's never about just grades or a contract to do better in school when your child is eighteen. Both are about independence and discipline. Discovering the moral of your story deepens your love and understanding for one another and also ensures this doesn't happen again.

> *"If you don't want to hear me talk, do what you're supposed to do and shut me up." -Brian Bakerism*

I admit, I was getting bold that summer. Originally, I wanted to go away to college with my godbrother. I imagined us living in the dorms away from home, studying and having fun. I thought this was the natural progression of things. However, when I was faced with the reality of what it would take to live away from home, I felt I had no choice. I admit I didn't give in peacefully, as one would say but eventually, I saw the wisdom in my parent's rules.

Pops was right. I had gotten cocky. I wanted to be more independent and I was bending the rules in an effort to be so. Like my dad said, he had raised a critical thinker, and this helped me to make my decision. I knew some of the things I was doing disappointed my parents, but I was also feeling disappointed that my steps into independence were thwarted. I was still feeling bitter the next day after signing the agreement when my dad asked me to go out to dinner with him. I had mixed feelings about this. We all know the hazy time after an emotionally intense argument. Things were raw. But we went and had a nice time. Later on, that same night, my dad wrote me a letter and I read it the next morning when I woke up. A copy of the letter follows.

In essence, it was a love letter from a father to his son. In it, he wrote of his love for me and how proud he was of me. At the end of the day, despite all of the hard feelings that had passed between us, I knew my father cared deeply about me. -Avery

Contract to live at off-campus University housing
8/7/13

- I will contribute to rent at the lofts.

- I will pay for school and books for the 1st semester

- You will maintain 3.5 GPA the 1st semester of school. If 3.5 GPA is not maintained, you will need to receive scholarships and or loans to attend the 2nd semester. The GPA requirement of at least a 3.5 will remain in place as long as I financially assist in any way shape or form during your college education. I will continue to pay for housing during the 2nd semester as long as you are in school.

- You will no longer have access to the car as you will be removed from the car insurance of all 3 cars that we own.

- Since food or a meal plan do not come with the rent, you are responsible for your food on a daily basis. I will not be providing any money towards your food budget. You can eat at home when you are around the house.

- The data plan will be changed on your phone to limit texting and internet access.

Avery Perry Baker   Date

Brian Baker   Date

Contact to stay at home
8/7/13

- You can remain at the house rent free as long as you are attending Sac State.

- I will continue to pay for your school and books.

- You will maintain a 3.5 GPA the 1st semester of school. If a 3.5 GPA is not maintained, you will need to receive scholarships and/or loans to attend the 2nd semester. The GPA requirement of at least a 3.5 will remain in place as long as I financially assist you during your college education.

- There will be weekly chores. If you fail to do them, privileges will be taken away accordingly. (I will determine on a case by case basis.)

- The data plan will be changed on your phone to limit texting and internet access.

- You can continue to have usage of the cars however you will pay $100 quarterly for insurance: Jan, April, Aug and Nov.

_____   _____
Avery Perry Baker   Date

_____   _____
Brian Baker   Date

Avery,

I really enjoyed hanging out with you last night. As I've told you before, a father cannot be more proud of his son than I am of you. I love and cherish the relationship we have and I look forward to watching you become the man that God intends for you to be. We are and have been very fortunate to share a bond as father and son that a great many people do not ever experience.

Today, there are so many broken relationships among families of color that the African American community is suffering more than ever before, and it's young black men right around your age that are becoming the worst victims of these broken relationships. I completely understand some of the frustration you must be feeling right now. I am and have become much more of an emotional person since Grampy and Uncle Mark have passed. The fact of the matter is that had it not been for you, your brother and your mother, I would not have made it through the storm.

Love,

Pops

The Long Road Back

"Saggy pants equal a saggy mind." -Brian Bakerism

We never let the boys get away with sagging their pants. "Saggy pants equal a saggy mind", I would tell them. I wanted them to be careful with the details. What's going on in the inside is often reflected on the outside and I didn't want them to send the wrong message out into the world.

I had lost so much in a very short amount of time. In less than two years, I lost my father, grandfather, grandmother and brother. I did what a lot of men do when things get hard, I got quiet, I put my head down, and I worked.

I tried to fill the emptiness by focusing on my job, and

when I came home, and I played the role of a dutiful father and husband. But I found myself merely going through the motions of day-to-day life.

During meals, I sat at the table with my family, but I wasn't really there. I thought I was doing my job by showing up and doing what I was supposed to do, but as each day passed, I found myself growing more and more distant. If I could get to the end of the day somehow making it through the basics, I considered it a win. Then, one day, even the basics weren't working for me. I was completely disconnected from my children, my wife, my friends, and most importantly, myself. It was too much.

My pants were sagging.

Okay, metaphorically speaking they were sagging, but I had withdrawn from so many things in my life that I no longer cared about the details. I was on autopilot as I navigated the waves of depression that grief brought with it. I was numb, in shock and lost all sense of feeling. Except fear. I couldn't imagine a future without my father. I was devastated, grief-stricken and afraid but most of all, I was heartbroken.

Thinking back, I realize I didn't fully understand why I was acting the way I was at the time. When you are overwhelmed with grief, anxiety creeps up and overtakes you. It overwhelms you in subtle, imperceptible ways until you don't recognize yourself. I didn't realize that I had withdrawn from my life, but others did. First, my family noticed and then my friends and finally my colleagues. I thought I was doing okay but, I wasn't fooling anyone. I thought that if I was accomplishing things, then I was doing okay.

I was wrong.

One day, as I was near rock bottom, a friend became concerned about my withdrawn state. She asked me if I had ever heard of a concept called "Emotional Intelligence." I was intrigued. I hadn't heard of it, so I did some research. As I began to read about emotional intelligence, I quickly understood that embracing this concept could help me get back to being me. I began to understand why I had been acting the way I was. It should have been obvious that I was deeply grieving. I should have allowed myself the space and time to heal. Pushing those feelings down and fulfilling my duties in a zombie-like fashion wasn't sustainable. I couldn't keep trying to outmaneuver my emotions. Eventually, like slow moving zombies, the feelings catch up with you.

Much of the information I read about emotional intelligence felt familiar to me. It dawned on me that the concepts were very similar to the values my parents had instilled in me. Self-awareness, empathy communication, collaboration, awareness of others, all these things were taught to me from an early age.

Gradually, I began emerging from the dark state I was in and began to regain control of my life. I started to come to terms with my grief and stopped trying to outrun it. I started to identify what triggered certain emotions, and more importantly I started to address them well before my emotions got the best of me. In many ways, it was the basic concepts of emotional intelligence that allowed me to course correct. Once again, I started to become the old me: an engaged boss and colleague, a loving husband and father, and a good friend.

I was trying to completely avoid the grieving process because for months, I had done it over and over again. I was still limping along, trying to protect the parts of me that were already wounded, when I was hit with another loss, and then another. Each time, I had to go through the process all over again. It was too much, and I broke down. Nothing worked.

After my brother died, a good friend gently told me

that as hard as it is, and as much as you may want to just go around, go over, or even under this, you can't. The only way to make it to the other side of grief is to lean into it. You must go through it if you hope to make it to the other side. My friend was right, there isn't a shortcut to grief.

Without some degree of emotional intelligence, we aren't aware of why we do the things we do, or why others do the things they do. I learned that emotional intelligence is made up of four factors and it's these factors that give us an intangible boost by expanding our awareness of the world around us. It's a powerful tool in our arsenal and a key to navigating the things that life throws at all of us.

Emotional intelligence is that "something" that makes us unique. It is also what helps us understand ourselves, and just as importantly, helps us to read and connect with others. When we are emotionally intelligent, we have genuine interest in others. These are skills that can be studied and developed and while we are on this path of discovery, we learn more about those we love and by extension, we learn about ourselves as well.

These are the lessons my parents taught me, and the very same keys that I teach my own sons. These are the principles that lifted me out of the hollow shell of grief I had retreated into and gave me the tools to find myself again. -Brian

Incorporating the tools of emotional intelligence will enrich our relationships and strengthen our bonds with those we care about. It will help us move through this world and enliven our understanding about our own character. Here are the tools we've discovered through research and good old-fashioned trial and error.

Self-awareness

To be truly emotionally intelligent we must first be self-aware. But what exactly is self-awareness? At its most basic, self-awareness is the ability to accurately perceive your own strengths, limitations, and emotions and to be able to monitor them in real time. This includes staying mindful of how you respond in challenging situations and how you respond to difficult people. This can be more of a challenge than it seems. Most of us like to think we know ourselves. We strive to balance family, work responsibilities and a social network. Some people even add other crazy things like exercise or hobbies into the mix. It's a lot to manage. Inevitably, challenging situations arise to distract us from all the things we are carefully juggling and once our anxious eyes look away, there it is — disaster! Balls drop! We lunge to catch one of the balls, but then, disaster again! Another ball drops! We scramble to pick up that one and, in the process, drop another.

And then another.

And yes, another.

In the midst of all this chaos, if we aren't self-aware, we probably think we can handle even more balls. Okay, we tell ourselves. Maybe I can handle another ball. Toss it here. I'll pick up those other ones I've dropped.

You know the drill.

This side-show of catastrophe goes on until we stop, and ask ourselves, "What in the world made us think we could keep these all up in the air anyway?" And why on earth did we need all of those balls anyway? Developing self-awareness will allow us to know our limits and when we know our limits, we never juggle more balls than we can handle.

Self-awareness displays both a healthy self-confidence

and a humility that is open to feedback and the perspectives of others. When we are self-aware, we know what makes us tick and we are comfortable with it. Others can see who we are and it helps them connect with us on a more authentic level.

When we are self-aware, we are keenly aware of our strengths. This doesn't mean we are egotistical or superior, simply that we know what we excel at and allow these gifts to better the world around us. We instinctively build on our strengths and in the process, push our limits. This is hard to do if we are unaware of our strengths and how we function on a basic level. It makes sense that if we want to develop deeper connections with our family, we must first connect with ourselves. So, how can we do this?

Keep a journal

The simplest of tools can be the most effective. A journal doesn't have to be a big production or take a lot of time. Unless you want it to, your journal doesn't even have to chronicle each day in detail. It can simply be a place to record thoughts, emotions, reactions, save ideas…anything. The important thing here is to chronicle the things that are important to you so you can look back and notice patterns in thoughts and behaviors to build upon or correct. You might also discover things you may not have known about yourself.

Look at yourself objectively

This isn't always easy or comfortable but learning to look at yourself objectively—seeing yourself as you really are—is important. It helps us to be more understanding and accepting of ourselves.

Here's a fun experiment: Ask some trusted friends to describe you and look at yourself through their eyes. Use what they have to say to expand your self-awareness. It may not be a comfortable exercise, especially if you have the brutally honest sort of friends, but it will help you to see yourself objectively.

Find quiet time

Finding quiet time to self-reflect is not as uncomplicated as it seems. We are surrounded by distractions that are much more alluring than our own thoughts. Our thoughts can be uncomfortable and so to escape them, we fill up our time with our phones, cable or social media. Our minds are seldom actually quiet.

When we are truly present in the moment we aren't distracted by less important things. We notice where we are and what a gift this moment is. We can't know ourselves if we can't even hear our own thoughts. Therefore, we need to find time to be quiet and listen to what we have to say about where we are, right here in this very sacred moment.

Self-management

Becoming emotionally intelligent requires us to not only be aware of our emotions, but also to manage them. However, self-management is often the most difficult thing to do. Managing projects, finances, and even other people, is easy compared to managing ourselves. Yet, self-management is directly tied to our ability to act upon and effectively manage our self-awareness. Think of it this way, we can only manage what we are aware of. When we are aware of our actions and the motivations behind them, we notice that little by little, we begin to manage our lives better. Our moods and our actions become more purposeful and effective.

Self-management encompasses learning several core competencies:

Behavioral self-control

Keep disruptive emotions in check. This is basic impulse control. When we have developed healthy self-awareness, we can sense when things begin to go off-track and we adjust our responses accordingly. This allows us to react appropriately to even the most difficult situations with restraint and respect because we aren't surprised by our emotions.

Resilience

In the face of setbacks, when we have dropped too many of those balls, perseverance and diligence are hallmarks of someone who knows that setbacks can be managed until things return to normal. Emotionally intelligent people are resilient in the storms of change and march right through them, knowing that the hardest parts in life are usually only for a short season.

Achievement Drive

On our path to becoming emotionally intelligent, we often notice something awesome begin to happen. Our ideas around what is "good enough" will begin to change and we begin to strive to meet higher standards of excellence. As this incredible change begins to take place, we will set out to achieve loftier goals and our lives begin to improve exponentially. We are no longer content with the minimum to just "get by." We will want more for ourselves because we have the self-awareness of what we are capable of. We discover that setting achievable, yet challenging goals enriches our lives and boosts our self-confidence.

Integrity

Emotionally intelligent people maintain high standards of honesty and ethics at all times. This integrity benefits all areas of our lives, especially in our relationships with our families, friends, and colleagues. All of these relationships are enriched when they know they can trust us. We need to understand that having integrity must begin with real honesty with ourselves. This integrity takes quite a bit of emotional courage. It takes guts to acknowledge our true feelings and desires without any self-judgement or fear or societal judgement. This self-work will help polish rough edges and allow us to embrace being a principled, honorable person to our core.

Personal Agility

Change is inevitable. It's not always welcome, but it's a sure bet that change will happen again and again in our lives. Emotional intelligence helps us to adapt to unavoidable changes. Personal agility is our ability to readily, willingly, rapidly and effectively anticipate and adapt to change.

If we haven't taken the time to develop this emotional agility, we become rigid and set in our ways. When we lack personal agility, we also tend to become fearful of change and feel paralyzed when change is thrust upon us. Self-aware people know how to respond to change, even if they are worried and fearful. It takes initiative to respond positively and to embrace change. We can help ourselves more effectively manage change by developing our strengths and managing our weaknesses so that we are in control of our emotional reactions in challenging situations.

Social/Other-Awareness

Social Awareness allows us to be able to read the "emotional mood of the room." When we cultivate emotional intelligence, we become aware of others' feelings, needs and concerns. It's this social awareness that allows us to connect with our families, friends and colleagues on a deeper level.

It helps us to understand one another and build long-lasting relationships based on trust and a mutual understanding. Developing social and other-awareness is a skill that can help us connect with people-even those with whom we can't seem to see eye-to-eye...on anything. You know, that one annoying coworker or the most stubborn of teenagers, or maybe their stubborn parents.

Connecting through social/other awareness encompasses

such competencies as:

Empathy

On the most basic of levels, empathy is the ability to understand the emotions of others. However, empathy is more than just understanding the emotions of others. If we take it deeper, empathy is also our ability to share the emotions of others, or rather, the experiences of others. Empathy is especially important when applied to our closest relationships because it has the ability to make the burden of difficult situations lighter for those we value the most. Through empathy, we walk a mile in someone else's shoes. It's what binds us together as humans because when we are shown sincere empathy, we realize that we aren't alone in our struggles.

Empathy is usually practiced in two basic steps. First, we sense the feelings of others and process the situation from their perspectives. This allows us to better appreciate their emotional state and align our emotions with theirs.

When we become emotionally intelligent, we understand how to share the emotions of another person. We don't take them on as our own, but we are taking an active interest in their concerns. We often say things like, "I've been there." Or, "I feel you." Or, "I get it." We nod understandingly in commiseration and place our hands on them in comfort. Sometimes, we've been at *that* level and we have *felt* what they are feeling.

We understand.

That being said, we don't have to experience the exact same things someone else experiences to have empathy. When we develop empathy, we can imagine what they are feeling. When we empathize with someone, we draw upon our own emotional memories to think about what they must be feeling, and we respond accordingly.

Avery demonstrated empathy at a very young age. He remembers how much sorrow it caused him to see me hurting. He demonstrated an innate emotional intelligence by knowing why I was acting differently.

> When our family experienced so many losses, my father became less patient with us. It was as if he no longer wanted to take the time to explain things. He was different and I didn't like it very much. Because this was such a profound change, I knew he was

hurting, and I honestly felt bad for him. I can recall one particular night, we were eating dinner as a family and my dad broke down in front of all of us. He apologized for how much he had changed since the deaths in our family. At that point, all resentment was put aside and I could do nothing but console my Pops. -Avery

Situational Awareness

Situational awareness is the ability to read a group's emotional currents. We've all had bosses that are unable do this, and we know how hard it can be to work in these situations. The same can be said for families. The ability to read "our" group's emotional currents will strengthen our bonds and allow trust to grow. Reading and responding appropriately to the unspoken signals of loved ones is a sign of a healthy relationship.

When we sense something is off, we first need to take a moment and observe why we are feeling the way we are. What is different? Ask questions. Observe. Being able to "size up" a situation and plan an appropriate response will also enhance our empathy skills.

Service Orientation

When we are developing our awareness of others, we become naturally more service orientated. We begin to anticipate and recognize the needs of others and we eagerly want to meet those needs. Becoming attuned in this way strengthens our connections as a family because we love those we serve.

Relationship Management

Relationship management is the social part of emotional intelligence. When we effectively manage our relationships, we become adept at inducing desirable responses in others. We don't do this to manipulate but rather to manage emotional situations. "Managing" a relationship sounds stiff and businesslike, as if HR should be involved, but in this case, what we actually mean is that we are positively managing emotional situations.

Strong relationship management allows us to relate with others and make difficult conversations productive. Emotionally intelligent people use clear and effective communication while providing timely and constructive feedback and genuine encouragement. This creates an individual style of inspirational leadership and loyalty.

Relationship management encompasses such competencies as:

Communication

Listening attentively and fostering open dialogue. We learned that the first keys in deeper connectivity is having healthy and open conversations. When we approach conversations with patience and love, we all win.

Interpersonal Effectiveness

Emotionally intelligent people possess natural diplomacy, tact and interpersonal skills. Because they know themselves and are confident in that knowledge, they relate well and build rapport with all people. They are comfortable in most situations they find themselves in and are eager to put others at ease as well.

Conflict Management

As we learned in the previous chapter, conflict management is an important key to fulfilling relationships. Negotiating and resolving disagreements within our families becomes easier when we develop our emotional intelligence and integrity.

Teamwork & Collaboration

Working with others toward shared goals is a source of joy and deepens the ties that bind us together. When we work together, we learn to trust and rely on our "team."

Coaching & Mentoring Others

Identifying others' developmental needs and in turn, bolstering their abilities is a hallmark of being emotionally intelligent. When we are confident in our own abilities and have experienced positive encouragement and coaching around our own strengths, we are able to extend this gift to others.

Bonds

We should always carefully tend to those bonds that we hold the most sacred and give us the greatest strengths. This is the most basic, and the most important thing to remember in managing our relationships. After all, isn't this why we are here?

I was thirteen when my uncle passed away. My dad knew that showing up in your Sunday best was part of paying proper respect to the memory of those we love, so he took me shopping for a new tie to wear to the memorial service.

As we were wandering around the racks of clothes, we talked about various things including how to choose a good tie. At some point, we noticed a man browsing through the racks close by. He seemed out of place among all the crisp colored shirts and neatly pressed slacks. He was disheveled and looked like he hadn't bathed in a while — a long while. He noticed my dad and I and approached us.

My dad smiled at him and nodded. The man gestured towards me and said to him, "Hey, I just want to tell you that your son is really lucky that he has a father teaching him how to shop." Pops' smile grew bigger as he thanked him. The man then leaned down to me and said, "You know, I remember when I was younger, my father taught me how to shave. That was one of the best times in my life." We talked with him for a minute and then he said, "Well, I'm here to shop for a funeral." I looked up at my dad and saw his face change. I realized we were all there for the same reason, and we all knew something of what the other must be feeling.

"I'm sorry to hear that," my dad said to him. I saw him glance down at the shirt the man was clutching. The bright, clean shirt made his pants look even more dingy and tattered. Pops hesitated for a split second before quietly asking, "Hey man, do you have enough money for that shirt?"

"Yeah, I have enough money for the shirt I got." He said. He shrugged and continued, "I guess I got to figure out where to get some money for some pants and a belt."

My dad didn't hesitate this time.

"Well, I tell you what." He said. "Why don't you go shopping and meet us downstairs at the cashier?"
"Really?"

"Yes, really." My dad assured him.

The man left to pick out a few things and we went downstairs to wait. Ten minutes later the man appeared with his pants, socks and belt in addition to his shirt. He was walking fast and looking around the store. When he saw us, relief etched his face and he came over to us with his armful of things. The cashier rang us up and we said goodbye to the man. I watched him go, carefully carrying his shopping bag of new clothes.

My dad later told me that he learned a long time ago that it's never a good idea to judge a book by its cover. The man could have had a lot of money, he told me. He didn't know, but what he did know right then was grief. He knew what the man must have been feeling. He felt it. He could also see the man was reaching out for some kind of human connection. He sensed the man could have used some help, so instead of reasoning away his intuition, he risked embarrassment.

My dad taught me an invaluable lesson the day he looked beyond a shabby appearance and instead listened to the voice of empathy. Though grieving himself, my dad took the time to ease someone else's burden for a moment and turned an unremarkable encounter with a stranger into a lesson of compassion and empathy that I would never forget. –Avery

FULL CIRCLE

Life is funny in the way it has of coming full circle. When we take a minute and think of where we've been, we can see how far we've come. We can also see it's never, ever been a straight line to where we are now. Heartache will inevitably come for us again, but then, so will joy.

If we are smart, we can take the lessons we've learned and apply them to whatever pops up to shock us out of our complacency. If we are smart, we recognize these obstacles as opportunities.

Right now, life is good.

Avery and I are having a blast sharing those hard-won lessons with people around the world. Justin is living his dream in Los Angeles and Lynette is working with a company she enjoys. We both take great satisfaction in watching our boys — young men now — pursue their passions. We stumbled over some hurdles that life threw in our way, but we all picked ourselves up, dusted off and kept going. There will be more hurdles. We know this.

When these hurdles show up, we will try to remember those lessons so that maybe we don't stay down as long. We hope we will bring our family around us instead of isolating ourselves. We will remember that we've worked hard to build trust through open conversations and how it's allowed us to resolve conflicts as we set aside our own pride and walked a mile or two in the shoes of someone we care about. Hopefully, we will also remember that empathy for ourselves is just as important as showing empathy for others.

We know that all of these keys that we now hold in our hearts will serve us and those we love better each time we use them. We know that when life carries us past the easier times and deposits us smack in the middle of the difficult ones, we will remember that even when it doesn't feel like it, Love Wins. Always.

BRIAN BAKERISMS

*Growing up, we heard these phrases so many times
we coined them, "Brian Bakerisms." -Avery*

"You are who you roll with."

"It's one thing to be the sh*t in high school, it's
another to be the sh*t in life."

"Closed mouths don't get fed."

"I don't care what other parents' kids can do;
other kids aren't my kids."

"Im'ma say this one last thing, then I'm going to
leave it alone."

"Be a leader, not a follower."

"If you don't want to hear me talk, do what you're
supposed to do and shut me up."

"Did you ask your mother?" *Yes, this is all dads.*

"The habits you have at 25 are those you start at 15."

"Don't be a masterpiece of minimalism."

"Touch with your eyes, not your hands."

"Saggy pants equal a saggy mind."

"You're gonna make mistakes, just don't make life altering mistakes."

"Be better on a Tuesday than you were on a Monday."

"You have two names. You have a first name and a last name. The first name is yours the last name is all of ours."

"We are just ordinary people with extraordinary relationships."

RESOURCES

Sometimes, you may need more help than can be found within the pages of our book, after all, we aren't medical or mental health professionals. If you find yourself in a situation that feels bleak and you don't know where to turn for help, please consider reaching out to these resources. Often, assistance is just a phone call away.

We are rooting for you!

The National Domestic Violence Hotline provides 24/7 crisis intervention, safety planning and information on domestic violence. Phone: 1-800-799-7233

The Suicide Prevention Lifeline connects callers to trained crisis counselors 24/7. There is also a chat function on their website. Phone: 1-800-273-8255

Anxiety and Depression Association of America (ADAA) provides information on prevention, treatment and symptoms of anxiety, depression and related conditions. Phone: 240-485-1001

SAMHSA Treatment Locator provides referrals to low cost/sliding scale mental health care, substance abuse and dual diagnosis treatment. Phone: 800-662-4357

2-1-1 Dial 2-1-1 from a local phone or use their website to search for organizations that offer community and local support resources and services.

For more information on Emotional Intelligence and Brian's training and certification, contact the Institute for Social and Emotional Intelligence in Denver, Colorado. http://the-isei.com

For more information on the link between social support and depression, see the following article:

Lakey, B., & Cronin, A. (2008). Low social support and major depression: Research, theory and methodological issues. In K. S. Dobson & D. J. A. Dozois (Eds.), Risk factors in depression (pp. 385-408). San Diego, CA, US: Elsevier Academic Press. **http://dx.doi.org/10.1016/B978-0-08-045078-0.00017-4**

Brian and Avery Baker are fast becoming one of the most inspirational father/son speaking duos in America. Their talks have been described as relatable, authentic, thought provoking, an experience, humorous, and relevant to the times.

And why is this?

While most parental and inspirational speakers simply tell parents, young adults, and teens what they need to do in order to have successful interactions and relationships, Avery and Brian share what they actually did and why it works.

Theirs is a real-life story with an uplifting message about what it takes to have healthy family relationships, parent/child bonds, trust and the ability to resolve conflict. Drawing from their experience of love, disappointment, joy and pain, they take the audience on a journey that is not only funny and heartfelt, but enlightening and informative.

They share the key factors that allowed Brian, old-school baby boomer parent, to close the generational divide with his new-school generational z child, despite the countless distracting forces that challenge today's families on a daily basis.

Families are more than a group of people who share the same last name or gene pool. Our families should be a source of love and encouragement and a haven from the rest of the world. However, we know that doesn't always happen. Sometimes, families go through rough patches while they navigate the same inevitable conflicts that all families deal with. In a lively and interactive discussion, Avery and Brian get real and honest while they share practical solutions to just how families can deal with these conflicts.

If you are interested in bringing The Avery and Brian Experience to speak at your family conference, corporate kickoff, college community, high school, or church retreat, please contact them below:

Phone: (916) 834-0292
Email: averyandbrianbaker@gmail.com
Connect online: www.averyandbrian.com